Life's
ENDLESS LESSONS

Life's
ENDLESS LESSONS

HIS.Precious.One

DEVINE DESTINY PUBLISHING
Milwaukee, WI

LIFE'S ENDLESS LESSONS

Divine Destiny Publishing, Milwaukee, WI

This is a work of non-fiction. All poems in this book are original works of the author. Any similarities to other works are coincidental.

Copyright © 2019 LaToya Barbee

All rights reserved. No part of this publication may be recorded, stored in a retrieval system, or transmitted in any form or by any means, electronic, mechanical, photocopied, recorded or otherwise, without prior written permission from the publisher.

ISBN-13: 978-0-578-53322-3

ISBN-10: 0-578-53322-7

Published by Divine Destiny Publishing

Milwaukee, WI

Printed in the United States of America

First Edition July 2019

Cover Design: Make Your Mark Publishing Solutions
Interior Layout: Make Your Mark Publishing Solutions
Editing: Make Your Mark Publishing Solutions

*I dedicate this book to my lifetime.
You, with God's help, gave me the inspiration,
courage, and strength to share my story. I hope
it will encourage you to share your story.*

"Come to me, all who are tired from carrying heavy loads and I will give you rest. Place my yoke over your shoulders, and learn from me, because I am gentle and humble. Then you will find rest for yourselves because my yoke is easy and my burden is light."

-Matthew 11: 28-30

Table of Contents

From the Author 11

Childhood 13
Dear Heavenly Father
Poems
A Letter to Toya

Military and Young Adult 33
Dear Heavenly Father
Poems
A Letter to Jordan

Ministry and Family 57
Dear Heavenly Father
Poems
A Letter to LaToya

Connect with HIS.Precious.One 89

From the Author

Writing poems is more than just releasing my sorrows and frustrations, expressing my joys and triumphs, or admitting my faults and failures. It's the expression I use to communicate to God. At times in my life, I couldn't verbally express myself, and my only outlet was through writing. I poured all my heart, soul, and being into my poems to God, but I never thought, one day, God would want me to share my poems with the world.

Three time periods in my life have shaped me into the woman I am today and made me look at life from different perspectives: my childhood, my military experience, and my family/ministry experiences. Each poem shows my mindset during those times. My childhood poems were written from a teen's perspective, from ages fourteen through eighteen. During my years in the service, I was ages nineteen through twenty-four. I wrote the family/ministry poems at ages twenty-five through thirty-four.

Each section begins with a prayer and ends with a poem, touching on several issues that affect our society, such as rejection, drug abuse, sex, depression, and suicide. The prayers include biblical scriptures, inspired to bring hope and encouragement. I also wrote letters to myself at each stage in my life to face my fears, forgive myself for past mistakes, and embrace all of me.

I learned that my life is not my own, and everything I go through is not just for me. My experiences are meant to encourage and uplift someone else, man or woman, boy or girl, young or old, rich or poor. I'm just a young lady who is under construction, a work in progress. My poems may not mean as much to everyone. However, I hope and pray, for whomever chooses to read my story, it will touch his or her heart with a desire to live. Even if it is just one person, I've done my job.

Childhood

Dear Heavenly Father,

Thank you for the gift of childhood. You tell us in Your Word we must come before You humbly as a child. A child's heart is pure, precious, and holy before You. A child is also a gift and an inheritance from You.

Not many of us reading this prayer had a good childhood. I pray for those who have experienced abuse, loss, grief, bullying, broken promises, rejection, abandonment, violence, and neglect. I ask You, in the name and blood of Jesus Christ, to heal our hearts, minds, bodies, souls, and spirits and begin the restoration process in our lives. You are the God of restoration, and You have the power and authority to redeem the time. Let us know You have sent Your one and only Son, Jesus Christ, to heal the broken hearted and forgive those who have wronged us. Help us forgive ourselves.

Your Word tells us to forgive those who have wronged us as You have forgiven our wrongdoing. Unforgiveness can hinder the blessings and promises You so desire to give us. Help us to let go, not for the offender but ourselves. I pray the Holy Spirit will release His presence, grace, comfort and, most of all, His love over us. Your Word says where there is the Spirit of the Lord, there is liberty. I thank You in advance for the victory we have in You. Continue to lead and guide us and reveal the divine purpose You have for us, filled with prosperity and not harm, hope and a future. Thank you, Heavenly Father, for Your unconditional love.

In the name and blood of Jesus, I pray. Amen.

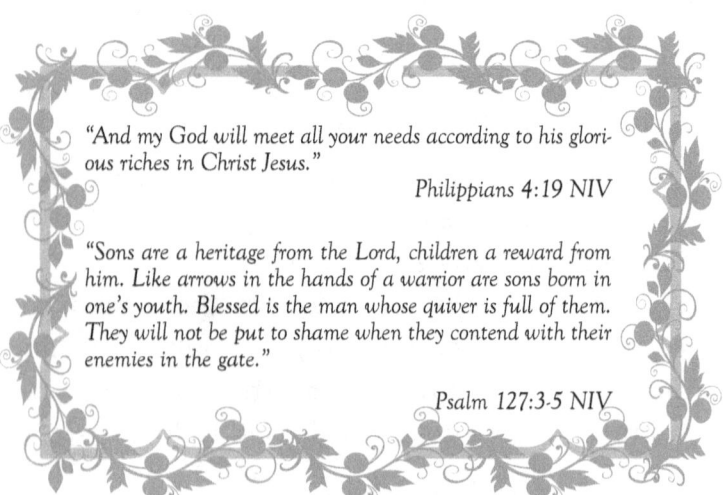

"And my God will meet all your needs according to his glorious riches in Christ Jesus."

Philippians 4:19 NIV

"Sons are a heritage from the Lord, children a reward from him. Like arrows in the hands of a warrior are sons born in one's youth. Blessed is the man whose quiver is full of them. They will not be put to shame when they contend with their enemies in the gate."

Psalm 127:3-5 NIV

Breathe Part 1

When God breathed into Adam, he became a living soul
The life given to me started out so cold
Being born from an adulterous relationship
I came out alive but ... breathless

This world had already labeled me a misfortune
Not knowing God's purpose for me was spoken
Walking around my family, acting like everything was fine
Not knowing my purpose had left me... breathless

I had to be the "perfect" daughter, since I was a deacon's kid
Singing in the choir, playing sports to win my parents' affection

Maybe now I can finally breathe
Wishful thinking ...

Compromising my innocence at thirteen caused my parents to shun me
Saying words like
"You stupid mother***"
"You can't wear white on your wedding day"
"You're not pure anymore"
"You won't be sweet when you turn sixteen"

The words spoken over me left me breathlessly rebellious
Not knowing God used my parents to push me toward my destiny
Promiscuously sneaky
I used my sweetness to get what I wanted
But I didn't enjoy it
It still left me ... breathless

(TO BE CONTINUED)

Love

What is love? Is it a feeling that just fell from the sky? Or is it a feeling only God can provide and understand because He is love? I'm tired of people using that word without meaning it because love is not a word that can just be said but a gift with which God has blessed His creation, and it comes from the heart. Love is more than flowers and candy. Love is greater than hate. Love is stronger than evil. And love is beautiful. Faith, hope, and love are the main gifts of the Holy Spirit, but without love, you can't have the other gifts. Love is not about saying it. It's about showing it. If you say, "I love you" and don't mean it, you have nothing but evil and the devil in your heart because he doesn't love God or us. All he wants is destruction. Be careful about what you say because it will come back to you hard. Love can cover a mountain of sins. Only God understands the power of love. Love. What a beautiful word. But it can be so ugly.

Thank You Jesus

Jesus, thank you for being the Lord of my life. Before I was even a thought, you were there with me. Thank you for being with my mom and me for those nine months. Thank you for being with me when I was conceived. Thank you for providing my parents the money they needed to cover my sister's and my needs. Thank you for being there when I had good moments and bad moments and bringing me through them. Thank you for giving my family and me a roof over our heads. You are the cream of my coffee, the comfort of my pain, the sun of my rainy days, the punisher and forgiver of all my sins. But most of all, thank you because by God the Father's grace, you died for me and forever You are praised. Amen.

A Prayer from the Heart
(Remix)

To God the Father I pray

His mercy will never fade away

To Jesus Christ I pray

His love for mankind will always stay

To the Holy Spirit I pray

His comfort will never delay

To the Trinity I pray

All man's sins they forgave

For help

In the ways of sin I stepped

To cleanse my mouth, actions, and thoughts

My hidden secrets, my hidden faults

Fill my mind with Your wisdom

HIS.Precious.One

The world says it's okay to practice Buddhism
Help me do what's right
Your heavenly glory shines so bright
But most of all, teach me Your love
The way to truth is from above
Amen, Amen, Amen

Victorious

Oh, merciful God, have mercy on me
I cannot breathe and bear it any longer
Please don't turn away, the need to be free
Forever, your righteous hand is stronger
As I cry, I do not know what to do
For my family and friends have turned away
Having nowhere to go, I turn to You
As Your Word says, Your grace will always stay
Although I'm unworthy to call Your name
Instead, You have chosen a soul like me
Your love for me will forever remain
Therefore, I am meant to be truly me
Lord Jesus, You are truly marvelous
In Your blood, I am made victorious

Why

Why am I feeling sorry for myself? Why do I feel so depressed? Why do I let things get to me? Why can't I just be happy for who I am? Why, when I want to do good, do I do evil? Why am I sinful? Why can't I please God? Why do my true enemies become my true friends, while my true friends become my true enemies? Why are people's hearts cold? Why are their eyes blind? Why are their ears deaf? Why do their mouths talk of violence? Why are their minds full of evil thoughts? Why can't people forgive and let go of the past?

I know the things people say and do hurt, but we must let those things go because we're better than that. What happened in the past is gone, and we should only be concerned with the now. The past hurts, but when I think about it, it gives me the strength to avoid repeating, with God's help. I pray to

Him every day that He'll be with me and watch over me. But I also want Him to be with my loved ones and enemies, for they are also sinful and in need of His grace. I don't understand why these things happen, but I've learned things happen for a reason, good or bad. I know in my heart God loves me and wants to save me.

Why am I asking these questions? Well, maybe because these are the questions some people ask, while others aren't concerned. I know I do. How about you? That's between you and God.

Can't Wait

I can't wait to go home, my real home, where there's no sin, pain, sorrow, death, and no evil. There will be happiness, joy, peace, love, and I will live for eternity. Oh Lord, I know it's going to be beautiful. The sidewalks will be covered with gold and so bright I'll see a reflection. Lord Jesus, please come soon. I'm sick of all the sorrow I'm enduring. I know I'm a sinner, and I deserve death, but by Your grace, you saved me, and I truly thank You. I'm tired of all the evil going on in the world today, and it seems like it's not getting better. Oh Lord, I pray that I'll be ready when You come to take me home. And I pray the people who don't know You will get to know You and receive You as their Lord and Savior. I pray that you'll be with the Christians and they'll be ready.

Shame

I feel ashamed of how I present myself to others. Some see me as an intelligent person, and some see me as a whore. Sometimes, I don't pay attention to it, but sometimes I believe it. I feel dirty from the outside and the inside but, most of all, because of how I fail to do God's will. I feel so lost. But someday, God will take all my shame away.

I Am Somebody

I am unique
I am somebody
I am special
I am somebody
I am beautiful
I am somebody
I am a leader
I am somebody
I am intelligent
I am somebody
I am a Child of God
I am somebody
I am great
I am somebody
I am healthy
I am somebody
I am full of hope
I am somebody
I am faithful to my Father in heaven
I am somebody
I am a dreamer
I am somebody
I am the future
I am somebody
I am a learner
I am somebody
I am a teacher
I am somebody
I am a fire for my people
I am somebody
I am the change
I am somebody
I am worthy
I am somebody
I am freedom
I am somebody
I am a believer
I am somebody
I am strong
I am somebody
I am love
I am somebody
I am here
I am somebody
I am me
I Am Somebody

Forgiveness

Dear Father in Heaven,

I come to You in prayer to ask You for forgiveness for myself and my loved ones, for we are not perfect in what we say, do, and think. And I ask You to help me forgive others as You forgive me. For the people I've sinned against, I pray You will help them find it in their hearts to forgive me. The time on earth is full of evil and violence. No matter how we treat people, there will be ones who will treat us wrong, even if we've done nothing to them. Even if we have realized our mistakes and asked for forgiveness, some people won't forgive us. I can't make them forgive me for all my sins, and I wish I could take them back, but I can't. I try not to think about those sins but, most of the time, I lie down and cry bitterly. I know I'm very sensitive and someone reading this poem my think I'm weak. But as I write this poem, my faith in God grows stronger. He lets me know He is always there for me. He does forgive me and wants me to be saved. As I finish my poem, I pray this prayer in Jesus' name. Amen.

God Is

God is good   God is kind   God is jealous   God is the end   God is great   God is the Creator   God is the answer   God is holy   God is everywhere   God is the Father   God is my strength   God is victory   God is hopeful   God is the Son   God is my redeemer   **God is love**   God is wonderful   God is the Holy Spirit   God is my rock   God is faithful   God is self-control   God is my refuge   God is trustworthy   God is my provider   God is my cornerstone   God is powerful   God is my shield   God is my best friend   God is righteous   God is my comfort   God is the judge   God is beautiful   God is peace   God is my husband   God is patient   God is shelter   God is my blessing   God is gentle   God is my prayer   God is salvation   God is justice   God is eternal   God is my healer   God is merciful   God is the Word   God is my deliverer   God is forgiving   God is my shepherd   God is my savior   God is joy   God is light   God is the beginning

A Letter To Toya

Hello Toya,

It's been a long time since we've last spoken to each other. I want to apologize to you. I'm sorry for the hurt you endured from the people you felt should have loved you and been there for you. I'm sorry for not knowing and understanding your worth. I'm sorry for the times you wanted to take your own life due to low self-esteem and rejection. I'm sorry for taking your youth for granted.

You are gifted, smart, intelligent, passionate, fun-loving, creative, sweet, loving, caring, and energetic. You have so much to give back to the world. God has fearfully and wonderfully made you in His image. He loves you so much and has created you to show His love to people through you. And you are loved.

Forgive yourself, Toya. Be free.

Military and Young Adulthood

Dear Heavenly Father,

Thank you for the honor and privilege to serve and protect our nation, the United States of America. It takes a special person to be willing to give his or her life to protect the freedoms we have today.

Many of my battle buddies and their families have suffered from the demands and stresses of the military. Some experienced depression, post-traumatic stress disorder, anger, suicide, physical injuries, family problems, alcoholism, racism, sexism, military sexual trauma, and more. I ask, in the name and blood of Jesus, to begin the healing process because carrying these loads is too much to bear. We are flesh and blood. We are not numbers. We have feelings. Help us realize that You are our five-star general, our supreme warrior, who is mighty in battle. You have never lost a battle and never will. You said in Your Word that we are more than conquerors in Christ Jesus, who loves us. You also said in Your Word "Greater is He who is in us than he who is in the world" (1 John 4:4 GW). Help us be the spiritual warriors You have called us to be for Your glory. Help us believe in ourselves the same way You believe in us. Jesus gave up His life for us, as many soldiers have given their lives for their families and nation. Thank you, Lord, for Your Son, Jesus. He made it possible for us to be victorious and fulfill the purpose and destiny You have for us.

In the name and blood of Jesus, I pray. Amen.

"I will not die but live and will proclaim what the Lord has done."
Psalm 118:17 NIV

"I can do all things through Christ which strenghtenenth me."
Philippians 4:13 KJV

"For he will command his angels concerning you, to guard you in all your ways."
Psalm 91:11 NIV

Breathe (Part 2)

Desiring to breathe

I thought maybe if I changed my scenery, I wouldn't live breathlessly anymore

I was dead wrong

My breathlessness followed me wherever I went

From college life to homeless shelter

Joining the Army was my ticket to a better me

Not knowing it would leave me more breathless

From failed relationships, MST, attempted suicides, mental hospitals, depression, deployment, PTSD, impulsiveness, rejection, racism, sexism, rebellion, drunkenness, becoming more promiscuous, lying, backstabbing

Even though I was breathlessly dead

God still breathed on me

Whoooo…LIVE…Whoooo…LIVE…Whoooo…**LIVE**

(TO BE CONTINUED)

Confession

So hurt by lies and tales of mankind

Falling in love can make a man go blind

Not just falling for a one night stand

Only God can measure a man's plan

Confused, frustrated, and depressed

Tired from all this unnecessary stress

Adding trouble on top of the trouble predestined for me to have

I can never blame a man for the mistakes I've made on my own behalf

God gives us free will while the devil lies, cheats, and steals

Back to the same old spell

Telling my side of the tale

It's been one hell of a ride

Many times, I had to get on my knees and cry

Don't know when the time will come to face my fate

Praying God will keep me from all this hate

Watching loved ones come and go before my eyes

But the memory of them will never die

So listen to what I have to say

There will be a time when my actions make their pay

May God shed His grace, peace, and, most of all, His love to us all

The day is coming when we will heed His call.

My Soul Cries

Although I am grieving
In God I am believing
Thoughts and memories fill my mind
Taking each day one at a time
Oh, Lord Jesus, how I want to enjoy my years on earth in Your glory
Telling my sad but encouraging story
About faith, hope, and love
In times of doubt, despair, and hate
Issues only God fully knows from above.

Don't give up, my soul
Your destiny was foretold
In heaven with God you belong
With your lips, praise Him with a new song
Let the Lord's will be done in you forever
Goodness and love are in His feathers.
Amen

Empty

Feeling empty

Don't know which way to go

Having so much to do but not having the funds to get it done at this time

God knows I need help

Sometimes I feel like I'm not in control of my life

I feel like I'm limited

But I know God doesn't have that in mind for me

I know I can take control of my destiny as long as it's in His will

There will be times when I can't control my circumstance

Lord, please give me the strength, courage, and wisdom I need to run my race

Please help me have peace of mind

Assure me that all things work together for my good
Because I love You and You chose me for Your good purpose
In Jesus' name, I pray
Amen

Can't Help But Wait

I can't help but wait to finally be the woman I was made to be

I can't help but wait to see the true me

I can't help but wait until I reach my destiny

I can't help but wait to see things in a godly perspective

I can't help but wait for the desires of my heart to come to pass

I can't help but wait for the man I'm in love with to marry me

I can't help but wait for God's will to be fulfilled in my life

I can't help but wait until I am financially secure

I can't help but wait until my mind, body, and soul are secure

I can't help but wait until I am in heaven and in Your arms

Can't help but wait

A Prayer Of Love

> "Love is patient. Love is kind. It does not envy. It does not boast. It is not proud. It is not rude. It is not self-seeking. It is not easily angered, and it keeps no record of wrongs. Love does not delight in evil but rejoices with the truth. It always protects, always trusts, always hopes, and always perseveres. Love never fails" (1 Corinthians 13: 4-8).

Love is not anxious (worry). Love is not selfish. It encourages, requires humility, and it sees the good in others. It is respectful. It is helpful. It is gentle (calm). It forgives. Love is honesty. It never harms, never betrays, never doubts, never gives up. Love prevails (conquers).

Lord Jesus, thank you for this precious gift of love. No one, including myself, fully understands it, but You teach and show us every day as long as we live. Forgive me, Lord, for the times I've misused it for my selfish reasons and took it for granted. I pray the people whose love I took for granted will forgive me and reconcile with me so there's no hatred in our hearts. And, Lord Jesus, I pray that I forgive myself so I can love myself and see myself the way You see me, Jesus. I know what I'm praying for is from the heart and You hear my prayer, a prayer of love. Help me forgive others and understand their actions and intentions. In Jesus' name and blood. Amen.

So Hard

So hard to love when the love you give isn't always returned

So hard to trust when you are betrayed by a close friend or loved one

So hard to dream when it's broken into pieces by life's circumstances

So hard to believe when life's struggles get the best of you

So hard to stay strong when you're backed against the wall by the issues of life

So hard to understand when all around you is confusion

So hard to accept when you don't want to be where you are in life

So hard to hope when no one seems to care

So hard to have faith when it seems like everyone and everything is against you

What do you do when life just gets so hard?

Pray, pray, pray

The Good Fight

There's so much in life I don't understand. All I know is to trust in God, believe in His Word, and live right. I will have to endure some tough times with the strength and courage found in God and my true loved ones. Anyone can say they care and they've got your back, but do they really? Not just other people but myself as well. I know I've hurt people and people have hurt me. I just pray the people I've hurt will have the heart to forgive me as I forgive those who hurt me. God sees all and knows all. He knows your heart. Love yourself as God loves you. And love everyone else, even if they don't like you or understand. It's not easy, but in the end, God will get the glory and save a lost soul. Don't give up. Fight the good fight.

Peace

As many thoughts are running through my head, wishing my life was different instead
A soft, gentle voice says …
Peace

Thoughts about my past and where I am today
Many thoughts running through my head, wishing my life was different instead
A soft, gentle voice continues to say…
Peace

My love, my hate, my joy, my shame
Many thoughts running through my head, wishing my life was different instead
A soft, gentle voice still says…
Peace

My disappointments, my hidden sins, my failures, ashamed of my hidden faults
All these are running through my head, wishing my life was different instead
A soft, gentle voice overtakes my thoughts…
Peace

Lord Jesus, You are my peace in a world so cold
You keep me at ease
Please don't leave me because, without You, I'm not at peace
Reassure me, Lord, that You are here
Your love is near
You have not given me the spirit of fear but of power, love, and a sound mind

So, Lord, I receive Your peace
My mind is now at ease

Tired

Lord Jesus,

I'm tired of crying …
Help me find peace in the circumstances I cannot control.

Hold On

Hold on (Love) Let it out (Forgive) Pray (Faith)
Hold on (Love) Let it out (Forgive) Pray (Faith)
Hold on (Love) Let it out (Forgive) Pray (Faith)
Hold on (Love) Let it out (Forgive) Pray (Faith)
Hold on (Love) Let it out (Forgive) Pray (Faith)
Hold on (Love) Let it out (Forgive) Pray (Faith)
Hold on (Love) Let it out (Forgive) Pray (Faith)
Hold on (Love) Let it out (Forgive) Pray (Faith)
Hold on (Love) Let it out (Forgive) Pray (Faith)
Hold on (Love) Let it out (Forgive) Pray (Faith)
Hold on (Love) Let it out (Forgive) Pray (Faith)
Hold on (Love) Let it out (Forgive) Pray (Faith)
Hold on (Love) Let it out (Forgive) Pray (Faith)
Hold on (Love) Let it out (Forgive) Pray (Faith)
Hold on (Love) Let it out (Forgive) Pray (Faith)

Hold on (Love) Let it out (Forgive) Pray (Faith)
Hold on (Love) Let it out (Forgive) Pray (Faith)
Hold on (Love) Let it out (Forgive) Pray (Faith)
Hold on (Love) Let it out (Forgive) Pray (Faith)
Hold on (Love) Let it out (Forgive) Pray (Faith)
Hold on (Love) Let it out (Forgive) Pray (Faith)
Hold on (Love) Let it out (Forgive) Pray (Faith)
Hold on (Love) Let it out (Forgive) Pray (Faith)
Hold on (Love) Let it out (Forgive) Pray (Faith)
Hold on (Love) Let it out (Forgive) Pray (Faith)
Hold on (Love) Let it out (Forgive) Pray (Faith)
Hold on (Love) Let it out (Forgive) Pray (Faith)
Hold on (Love) Let it out (Forgive) Pray (Faith)

Hold on... Let it out... Pray

A Letter To Jordan

Jordan,

You are not weak.
You've made some bad choices along this journey. But don't let those mistakes define you, who God has called and chosen you to be. You are a warrior. You are a leader. You are not just a number. It's okay to express your emotions.

Don't let other people's opinions of you make you question your self-worth. God made you worthy through the blood of Jesus. You are more than a conqueror in Christ Jesus, who loves you, who created you to do good works in advance for His glory.
Your life does matter.

Family and Ministry

Dear Heavenly Father,

Thank you for the gifts of life, ministry, and family. They are important to You.

Many of us have experienced divorce, abandonment, financial struggles, challenges when raising children, church hurt, trust issues, singlehood, disappointments, failures, and many others. Help us realize we cannot face these challenges on our own. We need You. You told us in Your Word to be strong and courageous because You are with us. You will never leave or forsake us. Transform our way of thinking into Your perspective, so we can see the good, perfect, and holy will You have for us. Help us trust You, Lord, and lean not to our own understanding. Guide and direct our footsteps. Your Word says a good man's steps are ordered by the Lord. You desire for us to live the abundant life You promised through Your Son, Jesus. We are Your masterpieces. Make us into the men and women of God you have ordained us to be for Your glory.

In the name and blood of Jesus, I pray. Amen.

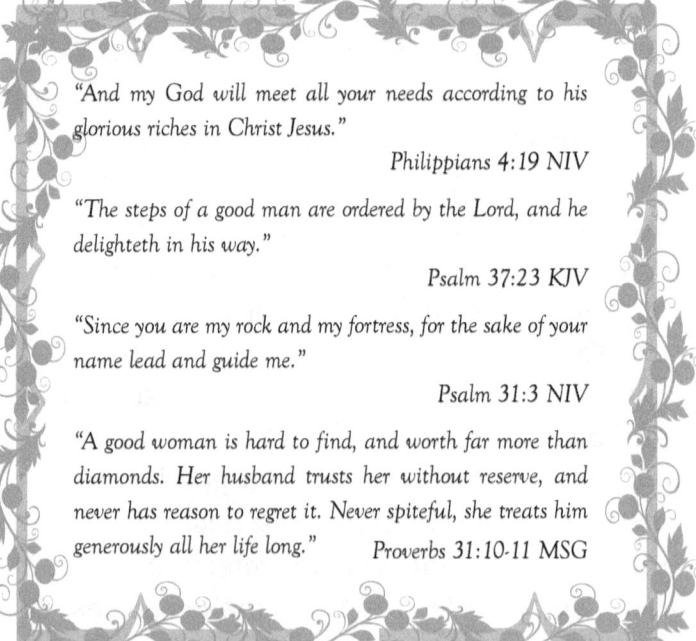

"And my God will meet all your needs according to his glorious riches in Christ Jesus."

Philippians 4:19 NIV

"The steps of a good man are ordered by the Lord, and he delighteth in his way."

Psalm 37:23 KJV

"Since you are my rock and my fortress, for the sake of your name lead and guide me."

Psalm 31:3 NIV

"A good woman is hard to find, and worth far more than diamonds. Her husband trusts her without reserve, and never has reason to regret it. Never spiteful, she treats him generously all her life long."   Proverbs 31:10-11 MSG

Breathe (Part 3)

Who would've known God had an assignment for me

My misfortunes pushed me toward my destiny

God sent a prophet to speak life over me

Saying God has a treasure box full of goodies just for me

Stay close to God and I will see

Everything in the treasure box will come to be

Calling me into ministry ... Wow!

Trusting me to reach His people

Married a preacher's kid and bore him a beautiful daughter

Knowing my purpose

Things started coming together

Now, I can finally breathe ... So I thought

Not knowing my breathlessness had a way of sneaking up

Financial struggles

Martial issues

Pregnancy complications

Self-identity struggles

Ministry burdens

So much to bear

My husband and I decided to sojourn to a new land

Thinking we could start fresh with new opportunities

Ignoring the warning before destruction

One month from having his daughter

Received his call that left me breathlessly torn

His words were around my neck

Choking me to death

Uhhh ... Can't breathe ... Uhhh ... Can't breathe ... Uhhh ... Can't breathe

His words killing me softly for the next six years

A wife raising our child alone

(TO BE CONTINUED)

Chosen. Crushed. Pressed. Refined. Released

Chosen by God

Crushed by others

Pressed by circumstances

Refined by adversity

Released into a life of supernatural prosperity and abundant living

LaToya

Loving, acceptance, truth, opportunity, youth, a child of the Most High God

At times, I couldn't live up to my name because I didn't know my worth. Being misunderstood by those I trusted, by those who said, "I love you" with their lips, but their actions said, "I hate you."

I've followed the wrong crowd and done some things I'm not proud of. I've told God I'm not worthy of His love and mercy because of my failures and shortcomings.

But God said to me...

You are not worthless. You are victorious. You are not useless. You are priceless. Your failures have made you strong through Me. Regardless of your shortcomings, I have directed your path. I have placed you where I want you to be. I love you as you are. Abide in Me as I abide in you.

"Charm is deceptive, and beauty does not last, but a woman who fears the Lord will be greatly praised" (Proverbs 31:30 NLT).

Unbreakably Beautiful

The force of nature I see is fire

Her flames dance gracefully with her light as bright as the sun

However, she is also as dangerous as a broken heart

With all her failures and disappointments, she is strikingly beautiful

Regardless of how destructive the fire was in her past

She is still unbreakably beautiful

Jehovah

Jehovah-Rapha
The Lord is my Healer

Jehovah-Jireh
The Lord is my Provider

Jehovah-Machsi
The Lord is my Refuge

Jehovah-Tsidkenu
The Lord is my Righteousness

Jehovah-Sabaoth
The Lord is my Strength

Jehovah-Shalom
The Lord is my Peace

Jehovah-Shammah
The Lord is Present and Ready to Save

Stuck

I know I'm not perfect and I've done some things that were wrong

But why did my husband abandon me?

Do I deserve this? Does our daughter deserve this?

All I wanted was a family, a husband who loves God, protects his wife, and provides for the family

Children who are loving and kind, who fear God, and are respectful and obedient

Is it just a fantasy?

Maybe I did marry the wrong man

Maybe I didn't belong in his family

I remember writing the qualities I wanted in a man in my poem "Godly Husband"

I don't know what to do

Maybe I didn't hear Your voice, Lord

Maybe they were just words, not Yours

I don't understand

If he really loved me, why did he do this to me?

A husband is supposed to love his wife as Christ loves the church

I feel stuck

Neighbor

So much in my heart I need to release

Casting all my cares to the Prince of Peace

Too much hate, too much pride

I don't want my love for people to die

It's really hard to find genuine and caring people

Loving your neighbor as yourself is not always simple

Especially when someone tries to put all the blame on you

While deep down inside, that person is hurting too

Heavenly Father, please heal our broken hearts

Putting our trust in You is a great start

As You mend our hearts and make us whole, please heal our souls

Teach us to see each other the way You see

The soul that each of us is meant to be

You are love

We are made from love

So we are love through You

So sweet and true

I love You, Lord

Forgive me for the times I fell short

I love my neighbor as well

Help me be a better sister and friend

In Jesus' name

Amen

Help Me

Heavenly Father,
Please help me! I'm so tired and frustrated with everything in my life, and I can't bear it anymore. Please take my burdens from me so I can be set free. Take my job, take my school, take my husband, take my mother, take my father, take my siblings, take my ministry. Take everything, Jesus! I'm tired of crying tears of sadness. I've done that all my life, and I need a change! Please perform a change in my life. You are not a man who should lie. Lord, please do this because I need You now! Your Word does not return to You empty. Please don't be a deaf ear to me.

Peace Be Still

In spite of my pain, sorrow, and tears

Peace be still

Missing my loved ones as I go through this journey

Peace be still

Facing my fears, insecurities, and past

Peace be still

Accepting the acceptance

Peace be still

Depending on God to lead and guide me on the right path

Peace be still

Pushing toward the mark

Peace be still

Seeing past my weaknesses

Peace be still

Walking toward my destiny

Peace be still

Becoming who I need to be

Peace be still

Breathe (Part 4)

While patiently waiting for the miracle of my husband's return, God, in His gentle manner, was telling me to let go

Feeling Breathless

Not understanding why my daughter was fatherless while trying to cover up my loneliness

Going to church to develop my gifts and serve God's people

Feeling breathlessly out of place within the congregation

With two college degrees and a good-paying job with benefits

Breathlessly hoping everything will work out

Became breathlessly tired, pressing me to say a prayer I didn't think I would

Letting go of the man I thought would be forever

Not knowing God has someone in mind to be my lifetime

Maybe ... just maybe ... I'll be able to breathe

Finding Myself

From saying, "I do"

To saying, "I'm divorced"

Never thought I would experience this

The sweet beginnings I miss

Not regretting eight years of finding myself

God used you indirectly in maturing me

The woman of God I am destined to be

God's will for my life is eternity

Thank you for the lessons I had to learn

Including giving me your last name and our daughter as a blessing

Our paths took a turn for a purpose

I apologize for the times I have let you down, not on purpose

HIS.Precious.One

There's a saying that time heals all wounds

I'm looking forward to the future

Letting go of my past and mistakes

Starting today, God's will and divine destiny for my life are now blooming

My Lifetime

I don't have many materialistic things to give you

I don't have a large number of followers on Facebook

I am just a young woman who's in love with you

Who sees the king in you

I can give you my loyalty

You can trust me with your secrets, and I will protect your heart with God's help

I will respect you and adore you

You light up my world just with your presence

I may not have the best body or the prettiest face

I can go before God in prayer, talking to Him about you and for you

Asking God to guide your footsteps, keep you from harm's way

And help you have a deeper relationship with God for yourself

Because God is the King of kings

I love you for who you are, unconditionally

You are my lifetime

My Past Is Anointed

My sister, through the Holy Spirit, told me last night that my past is anointed. She encouraged me to thank God for my past. Without my past, I wouldn't be the woman I am today. I wouldn't have met my true husband and had my daughter. I wouldn't have the courage to share my story. I wouldn't be the living testimony God can use to magnify His glory. Lord, thank you for my past. You've always been there with me, leading me, directing my footsteps. There were times I couldn't trace you, thinking I'd failed you. But you never left me. I am Yours. I love You so much. You called me a woman after Your own heart. You watch over me. You are the center of my joy. I want to fulfill my destiny, my purpose, my ministry for Your glory. Thank you for the gift of time. Time does truly bring healing with Your love, mercy, grace, and favor.

Thank you, Lord. In the name and blood of Jesus, I pray. Amen.

A Letter To LaToya

LaToya,

You have come a long way. I know this journey hasn't been easy. I'm proud of you. You are maturing into the woman of God He called, not who people wanted you to be. God does love you. You are His Precious One. His masterpiece.

Your new journey is just beginning.

Bonus Poem: Breathe (All Parts)

When God breathed into Adam, he became a living soul
The life given to me started out so cold
Being born from an adulterous relationship
I came out alive but ... breathless

This world had already labeled me a misfortune
Not knowing God's purpose for me was spoken
Walking around my family, acting like everything was fine
Not knowing my purpose had left me... breathless

I had to be the "perfect" daughter, since I was a deacon's kid
Singing in the choir, playing sports to win my parents' affection
Maybe now I can finally breathe
Wishful thinking ...

Compromising my innocence at thirteen caused my parents to shun me

Saying words like

"You stupid mother***"

"You can't wear white on your wedding day"

"You're not pure anymore"

"You won't be sweet when you turn sixteen"

The words spoken over me left me breathlessly rebellious

Not knowing God used my parents to push me toward my destiny

Promiscuously sneaky

I used my sweetness to get what I wanted

But I didn't enjoy it

It still left me ... breathless

Desiring to breathe

I thought maybe if I changed my scenery, I wouldn't live breathlessly anymore

I was dead wrong

My breathlessness followed me wherever I went

From college life to homeless shelter

Joining the Army was my ticket to a better me

Not knowing it would leave me more breathless

From failed relationships, MST, attempted suicides, mental hospitals, depression, deployment, PTSD, impulsiveness, rejection, racism, sexism, rebellion, drunkenness, becoming more promiscuous, lying, backstabbing

Even though I was breathlessly dead

God still breathed on me

Whoooo…LIVE…Whoooo…LIVE…Whoooo…**LIVE**

Who would've known God had an assignment for me

My misfortunes pushed me toward my destiny

God sent a prophet to speak life over me

Saying God has a treasure box full of goodies just for me

Stay close to God and I will see

Everything in the treasure box will come to be

Calling me into ministry … Wow!

Trusting me to reach His people

Married a preacher's kid and bore him a beautiful daughter

Knowing my purpose

Things started coming together

Now, I can finally breathe … So I thought

Not knowing my breathlessness had a way of sneaking up

Financial struggles

Martial issues

Pregnancy complications

Self-identity struggles

Ministry burdens

So much to bear

My husband and I decided to sojourn to a new land

Thinking we could start fresh with new opportunities

Ignoring the warning before destruction

One month from having his daughter

Received his call that left me breathlessly torn

His words were around my neck

Choking me to death

Uhhh ... Can't breathe ... Uhhh ... Can't breathe ... Uhhh ... Can't breathe

His words killing me softly for the next six years

A wife raising our child alone

While patiently waiting for the miracle of my husband's return, God, in His gentle manner, was telling me to let go

Feeling Breathless

Not understanding why my daughter was fatherless while trying to cover up my loneliness

Going to church to develop my gifts and serve God's people

Feeling breathlessly out of place within the congregation

With two college degrees and a good-paying job with benefits

Breathlessly hoping everything will work out

Became breathlessly tired, pressing me to say a prayer I didn't think I would

Letting go of the man I thought would be forever

Not knowing God has someone in mind to be my lifetime

Maybe ... just maybe ... I'll be able to breathe

Thank you for reading *Life's Endless Lessons*.
If you enjoyed this book of poetry, please leave
an online review. Thank you!

LEARN MORE ABOUT HIS.PRECIOUS.ONE
www.hispreciousone.com

CONNECT WITH HIS.PRECIOUS.ONE ONLINE
Facebook: http://facebook.com/latoya.barbee
Instagram: @his.precious.1

www.ingramcontent.com/pod-product-compliance
Lightning Source LLC
Chambersburg PA
CBHW021958290426
44108CB00012B/1122